IDEASHIP

IDEASHIP

How to Get Ideas Flowing in Your Workplace

JACK FOSTER

with illustrations by
LARRY CORBY

BK

BERRETT-KOEHLER PUBLISHERS, INC.
San Francisco

Berrett-Koehler Publishers, Inc.
235 Montgomery Street, Suite 650
San Francisco, CA 94104-2916
Tel: (415) 288-0260; Fax: (415) 362-2512; www.bkconnection.com

Ordering Information
Quantity sales. Special discounts are available on quantity purchases by corporations, associations, and others. For details, contact the "Special Sales Department" at the Berrett-Koehler address above.
Individual sales. Berrett-Koehler publications are available through most bookstores. They can also be ordered direct from Berrett-Koehler: Tel: (800) 929-2929; Fax: (802) 864-7626; www.bkconnection.com
Orders for college textbook/course adoption use. Please contact Berrett-Koehler: Tel: (800) 929-2929; Fax: (802) 864-7626.
Orders by U.S. trade bookstores and wholesalers. Please contact Publishers Group West, 1700 Fourth Street, Berkeley, CA 94710. Tel: (510) 528-1444; Fax: (510) 528-3444.

Printed in the United States of America
 Printed on acid-free and recycled paper that is composed of 50% recovered fiber, including 10% post consumer waste.

Library of Congress Cataloging-in-Publication Data
Foster, Jack, 1930–
    Ideaship : how to get ideas flowing in your workplace / by Jack Foster.
      p. cm.
    Includes bibliographical references and index.
    ISBN 1-57675-164-3
    1. Creative ability in business. 2. Psychology, Industrial. 3. Management. I. Title
HD53.F67 .2001
658.4'092—dc21   2001035912

First Edition
07 06 05 04 03 02 01   10 9 8 7 6 5 4 3 2 1

Copy Editor: Henrietta Bensussen
Indexer: Paula C. Durbin-Westby
Interior Design & Production: Linda Jupiter, Jupiter Productions

Jack Foster

To my wife, Nancy,
and my sons,
Mark and Tim

Larry Corby

To my daughter,
Laura Ann

CONTENTS

Preface   xi

Part I What Is Ideaship?   1

Part II How Do You Become an Ideaist?   5
  1. You help people think better of themselves   7
  2. You help create an environment that's fun   14

Part III Sixteen Personal Things You Can Do   19
  1. Follow the golden rule   21
  2. Care about the people you work with   24
  3. Remember that they work with you,
     not for you   27
  4. Make sure they like you   29
  5. Take the blame, give the praise away   32
  6. Hire only people you like   35
  7. Trust them   38
  8. Praise their efforts   40
  9. Allow them the freedom to fail   44
  10. Help them achieve their goals   46
  11. Never lie about anything important   48
  12. Show some enthusiasm   50
  13. Ask them to help you   52

14. Get rid of the word "I"   54

15. Play the fool   56

16. Have fun yourself.   58

Part IV Seven Organizational Things You Can Do   61

  1. Cut down on approvals   63

  2. Make everybody an owner   66

  3. Give them what they need   68

  4. Keep it small   70

  5. Tell them everything about their company   72

  6. Shun rules   74

  7. Pay for their education   76

Part V Eighteen Strategic Things You Can Do   79

  1. Don't ask for one solution — Ask for many   81

  2. Make their jobs seem easy   83

  3. Don't reject ideas — Ask for more   85

  4. Give them more than one problem at a time   88

  5. Ask for more ideas, sooner   91

  6. If it isn't working, change it   93

  7. Let them solo   95

  8. Let them do it their way   98

  9. Make sure the problem is the problem   100

10. Let them shine   103

11. Be wary of fear   105

12. Make it Us *vs* Them, not Us *vs* Us   107

13. Share what everybody does   110

14. Share experiences   112

15. Search for ways to create fun   114

16. Insist on vacations   116

17. Let them vacation when they want
    to vacation   118

18. Forget about efficiency, care about the idea   120

What Should You Do Next?   **123**

Notes   127

Index   131

About the Author   135

About the Illustrator   137

PREFACE

In my previous book — *How to Get Ideas* — I use James Webb Young's definition of an idea as "nothing more nor less than a new combination of old elements."

That definition, it seems to me, is a liberating one, for it says that ideas aren't some arcane things that only brilliant people come up with. Rather, ordinary people create ideas every day simply by combining things they already know about.

I also outline a five-step procedure for solving problems and getting ideas, a proven procedure that takes the mystery and anxiety out of the idea-generating process — (1) define the problem, (2) gather the information, (3) search for the idea, (4) forget about it, and (5) put the idea into action.

But I caution readers that if they want to get the ideas they are capable of getting, they have to first condition their minds by getting more inputs, by visualizing their goals, by trusting their child-like natures, by rethinking their thinking, by screwing up their courage, by learning how to combine, and, perhaps most important, by having fun and by becoming idea-prone.

As with so much in life, these mind-conditioning techniques are mostly things that we all have to do for ourselves.

But if you own or run a business, if you are a manager or a coordinator or a director or a supervisor or a department head, if you coach or teach or consult — indeed, if you hold any kind of leadership position anywhere — you can use your position to help bring out the creativity in the people you work with. How? Simply by helping them do those two most important mind-conditioning things — have fun and become idea-prone.

So that's what this book is about — *not* what my previous book was about, i.e., how *you* can get ideas; nor is it about how you can better lead or direct or manage or supervise the people you work with. Rather, *Ideaship* is about how you can help those people become great employees by unleashing their creativity.

Why is all this important?

It's hard to overstate the importance of creativity in the workplace, of having employees who bubble with ideas and solutions to problems. Indeed, Nathan Mhyrvold, former chief technology officer at Microsoft, says that a great employee is worth *1,000 times more* than an average one. The reason? Because of the quality of her ideas.

That's because new ideas are the wheels of progress. They drive the economy, they build businesses, they create jobs.

And great employees? Well, great employees come up with great ideas.

And why is this book unique?

The creative department of an advertising agency is unlike any other organization in the world because it is set up with only one purpose in mind — to create a barrage of workable ideas on a variety of problems for a variety of companies in a variety of fields.

Ideaship limns the lessons learned in such a department, lessons on how to create an idea-friendly environment and help people become idea-prone.

It then reveals a number of personal, organizational, and strategic things you can do to help unleash people's creativity and thereby get ideas flowing — as never before — in your workplace.

PART 1

WHAT IS IDEASHIP?

I spent half my life in advertising. Half of that time I ran creative departments in advertising agencies, half in creative departments run by others.

I was telling a client of mine one day about the difficulties of running such a department, a department that is — by definition and design — a collection of misfits and free spirits, of original thinkers, of people who resist authority and reject dogma; and whose strength is their ability to discover — on command — fresh solutions to a variety of problems.

He thought about it for a while, and then he said: "Running a creative department is not a do-able job. Any attempt to direct or lead or run people who are like that will be counter-productive. They'll rebel. Or they'll clam up."

Perhaps he was right.

But that's because we were using the wrong words. "Direct" or "lead" or "run" don't describe what I, and many like me, did.

We didn't direct or lead or run our departments. We ideaized them.

We weren't leaders. We were ideaists.

And the art form we practiced was not leadership. It was ideaship.

Henry Miller once wrote: "No man is great enough or wise enough for any of us to surrender our destiny to.

The only way in which anyone can lead us is to restore to us the belief in our own guidance."

A leader motivates and directs and runs and guides and leads. An ideaist restores.

A leader leads. An ideaist ideaizes.

In short, ideaship is a step beyond leadership, for an ideaist does more than lead — he or she restores to people their belief in their own guidance.

Another client of mine maintained that creative departments are so atypical that any lessons learned there about leadership (I hadn't yet coined the word ideaship) are not applicable to other groups of people in other kinds of organizations.

Phooey.

The creative people in advertising agencies don't have a patent on getting ideas. Everyday, the people you work with probably come up with dozens of ideas, from how to get to work quicker to how to stretch their lunch hours, from how to make deliveries faster to how to write memos better, from how to jazz up a sales meeting to how to speed up a production line.

So we know they *can* come up with ideas. And if you want them to come up with more and better ideas and with more original thinking and innovative approaches and fresh solutions, then an advertising agency creative department is far from some weird model that only a gull would emulate.

Rather, the reverse is true: It is a paragon for your organization, and the lessons learned there are a guide for you.

*   *   *   *   *   *

What follows then are some of the things I think I've learned and some of the conclusions I've drawn about ideaship from thirty-five years experience in advertising agency creative departments.

PART II

HOW DO YOU BECOME AN IDEAIST?

1.
YOU HELP PEOPLE THINK BETTER OF THEMSELVES

There are three reasons why it's vital for you to help people think better of themselves.

First, what people think about themselves is the single most important factor in their success.

Their personalities, their actions, how they get along with others, how they perform at work, their feelings, their beliefs, their dedication, their aspirations, even their talents and abilities are controlled by their self-images.

People act like the kind of persons they imagine themselves to be.

If they think of themselves as failures, they will probably become failures.

If they think of themselves as successful, they will probably become successful.

More to the point: If they think of themselves as creative, as fonts of ideas, they will probably become creative, they will probably become fonts of ideas.

"They can do it all because they think they can," said Virgil, and this fundamental fact about the triumph of self-image is as true today in business as it was two thousand years ago in Greece.

"Success or failure in business," wrote Walter Dill Scott, "is caused more by mental attitudes than by mental capabilities."

In other words, attitude is more important than facts.

The difference between people who crackle with ideas and those who don't has little to do with some innate ability to come up with ideas. It has to do with the belief that they can come up with ideas.

Those who believe they can, can; those who believe they can't, can't.

It's as simple as that. And it's no longer open to question.

If you doubt it, just ask yourself why so many seemingly gifted people fail, and why so many seemingly impoverished people succeed.

It's not because of who they are. It's because of who they think they are.

Second, what William James called "the greatest discovery of my generation" is also a fact. The discovery?

"Human beings can alter their lives by altering their attitudes."

Or as Jean Paul Sartre put it: "Man is nothing else but what he makes of himself."

This too is no longer open to question.

And yet this is what many leaders refuse to accept. And as long as they refuse to accept it, they will never become ideaists.

They accept that people's self-images drive their lives but — despite all the evidence cited by parents, by clergymen, by doctors, by philosophers, by psychologists, by teachers, by therapists, and by the hundreds of self-improvement books — they reject the notion that those same people can *change* their self-images.

They accept "As a man thinketh in his heart, so is he." But they seem to think that if a man thinketh differently in his heart he will remain the same man.

He won't. He will be a different man.

Or they seem to think that a man *can't* think differently in his heart, that the way he thinks today is locked in stone forever.

They are wrong. He *can* think differently.

Everybody accepts now that the mind can alter how the body works. The evidence that it can and does is simply overwhelming.

Drug addicts take placebos and have no withdrawal symptoms, allergy sufferers sneeze at plastic flowers, unloved children physically stop growing, hypnotized patients undergo surgery without anesthesia, people lower their blood pressures and heart rates by willing it, cancer victims experience spontaneous remissions, hopeless cripples walk away from Lourdes cured — the examples are legion.

But accepting the concept that the mind can alter the body is a huge leap, a major leap, perhaps even a quantum leap.

All I'm asking you to accept is a minor leap — that the mind can alter the mind.

Indeed, if you are to become an ideaist, you must accept that the people you work with can and must change.

Otherwise, you are doomed to lead a stagnant, never-improving company, a company that will probably end up where it began — at the bottom.

Third, because of your position as an ideaist, you can help the people you work with alter their attitudes.

Indeed, that is your primary job —

to help people think better of themselves,

to help them raise their self-images.

And you do it, not by commanding, but by restoring; not by directing, but by unleashing; not by leading, but by ideaizing.

Let me tell you a story:

I once worked at Foote, Cone & Belding in Los Angeles as a copywriter. Working with me was another copywriter named Glenn. He was an older guy who was a sweetheart of a person, and — when he put his mind to it — a brilliant writer. The problem was that Glenn had lost it — he drank a lot and didn't do much. And when he did do something, his ideas for ads were hopelessly old-fashioned, his copy rambling and disjointed.

I left that agency about the time that John O'Toole, the legendary ad man, arrived as creative director. Two years later, John was promoted to creative director of Foote, Cone in Chicago, and I returned and took over his job in Los Angeles — only to learn that Glenn was still there. But, to my surprise, it was the brilliant Glenn, not the lost one. From my first day as creative director, he was great — coming up with good ideas, writing well, not drinking.

I phoned John and asked him what happened.

"Well, I knew Glenn was a fine writer," he said. "He'd just lost his confidence, that's all. So I told him I thought that he was the best writer I knew and asked him if he would please edit the things I wrote. Every ad, every presentation, every memo, every proposal, every letter, I showed to Glenn first and asked for his help in making them better. It only took about a month before he was back to his old self."

John had restored. John had unleashed. John had ideaized.

Once you accept that as the ideaist's role, it colors everything you do — who you hire, the kind of environment you create, the directions you give, the way you give directions, how you set up your company, your systems, your procedures, how you deal with people, your training programs, what kind of clients and customers you attract, your goals, what you produce, the kind of service you give, everything.

For your company is only a vehicle for you to achieve your goals.

After all, it cannot have any goals of its own — it is only a reflection of you and the other people who set it up and run it. Its goals are your goals.

And as soon as you accept that *your* primary goal is to help people think better of themselves — to inspire and unleash and restore — you must accept that the primary goal of your company cannot be to make more money or better products, or to produce better work, or to deliver better service.

Its primary goal must be *your* primary goal — to help people think better of themselves, and to provide the kind of environment in which inspiring and unleashing and restoring can flourish.

If creating that kind of environment is the primary goal, then the other more traditional goals — like delivering better service, like making more money and better products — will come naturally, for when you achieve this goal, the people you work with will provide more and better service, and will produce more and better ideas and work; and they will do it faster and more efficiently.

But, you ask, specifically what kind of environment do you create?

2.
YOU HELP CREATE AN ENVIRONMENT THAT'S FUN

If you are to make people think better of themselves, the environment must be friendly instead of hostile, open instead of closed, supportive instead of discouraging, relaxed instead of rigid, inclusive instead of divisive — all the things that all the books on leadership and empowerment espouse.

But it must be more than that.

If you want ideas to flourish, it must be fun.

"Make it fun to work at your agency," wrote David Ogilvy. "When people aren't having any fun, they seldom produce good advertising. Kill grimness with laughter. Encourage exuberance."

Mr. Ogilvy did not have to limit his remarks to advertising agencies and advertising. The same could be said about any kind of business producing any kind of product or service. For you know it's true:

People who have fun doing what they're doing, do it better.

"The number one premise in business is that it need not be boring or dull," said Thomas J. Peters. "It ought to be fun. If it's not fun, you're wasting your life."

Note that neither Ogilvy nor Peters had any doubt about which is the more important — good work or fun. The fun comes first.

"If you ask me what is our primary purpose," said Ogilvy, "I would say that it is not to make the maximum profit for our shareholders, but to run our agency in such a way that *our employees are happy*. Everything follows from that — good work, and good service to clients."

My experience tells me what Ogilvy's experience told him — people do good work because they're happy, because they're having fun, not vice versa.

Granted, they have a sense of accomplishment, and they feel pleased and fulfilled when they do good work; but — at least among the writers and art directors in the advertising agencies I worked in — those feelings do not seem to carry over to the next job, or to the next.

Fun does.

Fun, like enthusiasm, is contagious and has a snowball effect that helps generate good work over and over again throughout the organization.

This was proven to me early in my career.

When I started in advertising, the writers and art directors dressed the way everybody in business dressed — the men wore suits and ties; the women, dresses or suits.

In the late '60's all that changed. People started dressing in sweaters and blue jeans and T-shirts and tennis shoes. I was running a creative department then, and the *Los Angeles Times* asked me what I thought about people coming to work like that.

"I don't care if they come to work in their pajamas," I said, "as long as they get the work out."

Sure enough, the day after the article (with my quote) appeared, my entire department showed up in pajamas.

It was great fun. The office rocked with laughter and joy.

More important, that day and the weeks that followed were some of the most productive times my department ever had. People were having fun, and the work got better.

Note again the cause and effect relationship: The fun came first; the better work, second. Having fun unleashes creativity. It is one of the seeds you plant to get ideas.

Indeed, *nothing is more important for an ideaist to do* than to create this kind of an environment, an environment where people enjoy coming to work everyday, where there's a feeling of camaraderie and good fellowship, where people attack their work with alacrity and confidence, where they like the people they work with, where they think of themselves as partners instead of employees, where — in short — it's fun to work.

When this happens, the work ceases to be a drag and takes on an effortless, easy-flowing, natural, Zen-like quality that results in more solutions, fresher solutions, better solutions, easier and faster.

The authors of *301 Ways to Have Fun at Work* agree. Dave Hemsath and Leslie Yerkes wrote, "We believe that fun at work may be the single most important trait of a highly effective and successful organization; we see a direct link between fun at work and employee creativity, productivity, morale, satisfaction, and retention, as well as customer service and many other factors that determine business success."

So too does the philosopher Alan Watts: "Don't make a distinction between work and play," he wrote, "and don't imagine for one minute that you've got to be serious about it."

* * * * * *

What follows are some suggestions on how to help the people you work with believe in themselves, and how to create the kind of environment that encourages that kind of belief — suggestions, in short, on how to get them to come up with more and better ideas.

If any of the suggestions don't make sense to you or don't set well with you, disregard them.

Be your own kind of ideaist, not someone else's. Follow your own gut feelings, not someone else's.

Here's why:

First, if you don't feel good doing something — if it isn't easy and natural for you — you probably won't do it well. And if you don't do it well, it probably won't work, no matter how "right" it is.

Second, when you do something someone else's way and you succeed, you never know if you also would have succeeded doing it your way. And if you fail, you never know either. It is a lose-lose situation.

On the other hand, when you do it your way and you succeed or fail, it is a win-win situation, for you know that it was because of you, not someone else, that you succeeded or failed.

PART III

SIXTEEN PERSONAL THINGS YOU CAN DO

1.
FOLLOW THE
GOLDEN RULE

It is more than a lesson in morality and a guide for getting along. It is a cardinal principle of ideaship.

All the good people you work with believe they can do more. Much more.

Indeed, most dream of running the company, or at least some department in the company, just as you did when you were in their positions.

Most dream of coming up with ideas that will invigorate or revolutionize the company, just as you did when you were in their positions.

The way you wanted to be treated then is the way they want to be treated now.

You didn't want to be treated as a servant or a follower, as a person who could not think but only take orders. Neither do they.

Instead, you wanted to be treated as the person you would one day become. You wanted your boss to see the potential within you.

So do they. And just as you are only as good as you think you are, so are they.

You must help make the people you work with believe in their greatness. Unless they do, they will never attain it.

In short, if you want them to explode with creativity and attack their work with alacrity, you must treat them not as slugs, but as people who bubble with ideas.

"When we treat a man as he is," Goethe wrote, "we make him worse than he is. When we treat him as if he already were what he potentially could be, we make him what he should be."

2.

CARE ABOUT
THE PEOPLE
YOU WORK WITH

Remember that the people you work with are not workers or helpers or assistants or trainees or lackeys or gofers or employees or inferiors or superiors. They are people. And if you think of them as people — separate, important, unique human beings — they will sense it and will respond by trusting you, by helping you, by accepting your suggestions, even by forgiving your blunders.

Indeed, if people believe that you are acting in their best interests, they will support your actions, even if what you are doing is not in their best interests.

But if people do not believe what you are doing is in their best interests, they will not support your actions, even if what you are doing is in their best interests.

None of this can be faked, save by a consummate actor, which you probably are not. It must come from the heart. You must care about them as people. You must like them. If you cannot, forget about becoming an ideaist now before you waste half a lifetime striving only to ultimately fail.

Of course some people in management positions feel they should remain aloof from their "troops," that getting to know them personally weakens their authority and limits their ability to lead.

Phooey.

Nothing could be further from the truth. Nobody save a goose follows a stranger. And nobody, not even a loon, is inspired by aloofness. When companies that are run by strangers actually do succeed, it is in spite of them, not because of them.

After all, do you want to work with someone who doesn't give a damn about you?

Then why do you think others do?

Ideaists open doors and tear down walls. They care. And people who work with them know they care because they give of themselves.

Unapproachable leaders who hide in their offices, who neither mingle nor probe, who protect themselves with the shield of authority — they are not ideaists. They are not even leaders. They are directors.

A friend of mine who worked in a big advertising agency in New York told me this story:

"We had over a hundred writers and art directors in the creative department when the executive creative director got himself fired. A lot of us regular creative directors wanted his job — heck, a lot of us were qualified for the job — but the top guns went out and hired a woman from a hot-shot agency in California instead. Naturally, we all resented her. But she won us over instantly by doing one simple thing — on her first day at work, she had the door to her office removed and taken down to the basement."

Talk about tearing down walls!

3.
REMEMBER THAT THEY WORK WITH YOU, NOT FOR YOU

You must ideaize, not through the force and strength of your position, but through the force and strength of your character, your ideas, your vision, your drive, your enthusiasm.

The people you work with should *want* to help you, not have to help you.

There is a practical reason for this: Work generated by command never has the freshness or spontaneity of work generated by desire.

True, forced labor is a good way of breaking rocks, but it seldom breaks new ground. And yours is a business of breaking new ground, an endeavor that requires what only desire can generate — freshness and spontaneity.

4.
MAKE SURE
THEY LIKE
YOU

That old saying about not caring whether people like you or not just as long as they respect you is one of those rules that may have worked in yesterday's military, but it has no place in today's business.

Certainly you must earn the respect of the people you work with. That's a given.

But make no mistake about it — you are running a popularity contest, for it is simply no fun to work with someone you dislike.

And when people aren't having fun, work becomes work, and thus drudgery, and thus uninspired.

Happily enough, it is easy to make sure that the people you work with like you.

Simply make sure that you like them.

Over and over again in my career, I saw proof of the power of liking people.

Large creative departments in advertising agencies are usually comprised of groups of writers and art directors. These groups are headed by creative directors. During the course of a year, switching often occurs among the groups, with art director A going from Group X to Group Y; writer B, from Group C to Group D, and so on.

I saw again and again that when a writer or art director or producer switched from a group headed by an unpopular creative director to a group headed by a popular one, he or she started doing better work.

So don't tell me that being liked is overrated. I know better.

5.
TAKE THE BLAME,
GIVE THE PRAISE
AWAY

In your position as ideaist, you'll be blamed when things go wrong, and you'll be praised when things go right.

First, take the blame.

After all, it probably is your fault. You assigned the work. You hired the people who did the work. You helped train them. You helped set up the systems and procedures they followed. You helped create the environment they worked in. If they didn't do the job well, it's at least as much your fault as it is theirs.

And even if it isn't your fault, blaming others lessens everyone — you and the ones you blame. It is a lose-lose situation.

Taking the blame is a win-win situation.

Besides, if you don't accept the blame you'll be secretly scorned by those above and below you, so you might as well own up to it and get on with your life.

Second, give the praise away.

If you don't, you'll be secretly resented by everybody who worked with you on the project.

Besides, the more you give it away, the more people will think you're just being modest; the more you *don't* give it away, the more they'll think you're just being greedy and egotistical.

Let me tell you a story:

In 1901, Mrs. Anna Edson Taylor became the first person to go over Niagara Falls in a barrel and live to talk about it.

And talk she did.

She talked at teas and luncheons and dinners, at bridge clubs and sewing bees, at political meetings and business meetings and union meetings. She talked to newspaper columnists and magazine editors. If there was a soapbox sitting around anywhere, Mrs. Taylor stepped up on it and started talking about her death-defying trip over the Falls.

Finally, the good old *Denver Republican* had enough of it. "It seems to us," the *Republican* commented editorially, "that Mrs. Taylor is taking a lot of credit that rightly belongs to the barrel."

You've got a barrel. Never forget to talk about it.

6.
HIRE ONLY PEOPLE YOU LIKE

No matter what their resumes say; no matter how many degrees or honors or awards they have; no matter their parents, their teachers, their mentors, their education, their job experiences, their contacts, their business associates; no matter how good their previous work; no matter how much they know, or how well they talk or write or present or handle themselves; no matter how glowing their references and accomplishments; no matter how perfectly they seem to fit the jobs you have to fill; no matter where they went to school, or what they've done, or who they know, or where they've worked, or who they've worked with, or what they've worked on — if you don't like them, if you don't feel comfortable and at ease with them, if you don't think you could drive across the country with them in a Volkswagen Beetle, don't hire them.

If you do, you will eventually have a problem. Guaranteed.

They will not be fun for you or other people to work with. They will not add to the camaraderie that is essential when people work closely with things as fragile as ideas.

Instead, they will eventually poison the most important thing you can create if you want ideas to flow — the environment of your company.

This is not to say that everybody you like will work out. Of course they won't. It is only to say that nobody you dislike will. Guaranteed.

Having found someone you like, what else must you look for?

Look for curious people, people who are interested in all sorts of things, people whose knowledge is horizontal rather than vertical.

Look for people who can get along with the people they will be working with. Remember that in any team activity, chemistry is more important than talent. So have a number of people interview (or at least talk to) them too. If some of them don't like the new person, beware.

Look for people who are up, who laugh, who like to play, who have a sense of humor. "Serious people have few ideas," wrote Paul Valéry. "People with ideas are never serious."

Look for fire. Look for pride. Look for the desire to make a mark. Look for the willingness to give in order to get.

Look for people who break rules, people who frighten you with the audacity and originality of their ideas.

Look for a sense of dis-ease with the way things are, and an urge, even a compulsion, to change them. For neither your business nor the world is ever changed by people who are content with the status quo.

People who accept instead of question, who smooth instead of rock — these people seldom make creative breakthroughs, because they follow and imitate.

And your job is to restore to people the belief in their own guidance and their own creativity, and thus have people who lead themselves.

7.
TRUST
THEM

"Trust men, and they will be true to you," wrote Emerson. "Trust them greatly, and they will show themselves great."

Doubt them, and they start doubting themselves. And nothing breeds failure like doubt.

Indeed, when they learn that you trust them to do a job they themselves might not think they *are* capable of doing, it will help them think that they are capable of doing it. It will help them raise their self-images; and from that moment on, they will start performing at a new, higher level.

Of course this does not mean that you should hand them a job and then walk away. You must monitor their progress regularly.

But you must also make it clear to them that it is their job, not yours, and that you trust them to do it well.

8.
PRAISE
THEIR
EFFORTS

"Appreciation is to talent," wrote Baltasar Gracian in 1653, "what the West wind is to flowers — life and breath itself."

"I have yet to find the man," wrote Charles Schwab, "however exalted his station, who did not do better work and put forth greater efforts under a spirit of approval than under a spirit of criticism."

"A great manager," said Reggie Jackson, "has a knack of making ballplayers think they are better than they think they are. He forces you to have a good opinion of yourself. He lets you know he believes in you. And once you know how good you really are, you never settle for playing anything less than your very best."

"One thing scientists have discovered," wrote Thomas Dreier, "is that often-praised children become more intelligent than often-blamed ones. There's a creative element in praise."

All these people and thousands like them have recognized the same thing — praise makes people better.

But some leaders feel praise should be meted out grudgingly, and only occasionally, and only if richly deserved; that too much praise lessens its effect, that each accolade makes the next one less meaningful, that bosses should be hard to please and stingy with compliments.

Phooey.

That kind of attitude will never develop people who generate ideas.

As long as you keep it specific, you cannot praise too much. It is impossible. The need most people have for sincere, honest praise is insatiable.

Do you ever tire of being complimented? Then why do you think others would?

Nor does too much praise lessen its effect. People want to believe in themselves. Praise helps them do it. Perhaps the people you work with will someday no longer need reassurance. But don't hold your breath.

Nor is praise from one who seldom gives it more beneficial than praise from one who gives it a lot.

Granted: Hard-to-get praise carries more impact than easy-to-get praise.

But the holding back of praise carries even greater impact, for it is always damaging and often disastrous. It makes people think their work is being taken for granted, that their jobs don't matter, that what they produce doesn't matter. It makes them feel unappreciated and unrecognized. It causes anger and resentment.

Worst of all, it lowers self-images.

In sum: An ideaist's primary job is to make people believe in themselves. Someone who seldom gives praise makes people doubt themselves.

None of this is to suggest that you must run around wildly giving out compliments, only that you must never hold them back.

Furthermore, you must look for ways of giving compliments often. And remember — every day is not too often.

It certainly isn't for John Ball, the Service Training Manager of American Honda Motor Company. Every day, he tries "to remember that . . . people may actually need day-to-day praise and thanks for the job they do. I try to remember to get up out of my chair, turn off my computer, go sit or stand next to them and see what they're doing, ask about the challenges, find out if they need additional help, offer that help if possible, and, most of all, tell them in all honesty that what they are doing is important: To me, to the company, and to our customers."

9.
ALLOW THEM THE FREEDOM TO FAIL

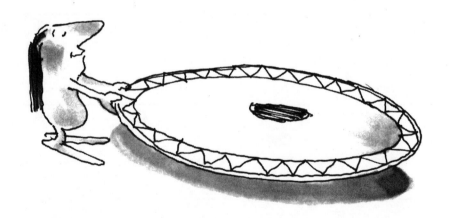

It doesn't take a genius to praise people when they do a great job. Even poor leaders are smart enough to do that.

The ideaist looks for ways to praise them when they fail. For this is when people are most vulnerable. This is when their self-images can take a nosedive.

Remember, one of the reasons good people are good is that they believe in themselves and in their ideas, they take chances, they swing for the fences. Criticize them or make no comment when they strike out, and they'll start trying to punch the ball into right field.

When they go for broke, praise them for the effort, for trying to do something others might not even attempt, whether they hit the ball or not.

I realize that this advice flies in the face of that old management dictum that you should "never confuse efforts with results."

But results seldom happen without effort. And my experience with creative people convinces me that if you don't acknowledge and praise effort, it will eventually wither like an unwatered flower.

10.
HELP THEM ACHIEVE THEIR GOALS

Napoleon, they say, never asked his men to win a battle. That was what *he* wanted. Instead of victory he promised them food when they were hungry, furloughs when they were homesick, recognition when they were forgotten, rest when they were weary, shelter when they were cold.

In the same way, you should avoid trumpeting corporate goals. "We'll be one of the biggest agencies in town" may well be what you want. But "You'll be rich and famous" may well be what they want.

At least once a year, sit down with people and find out what they want. Then work with them on achieving those wants and goals and aspirations.

I remember being stunned during one such meeting to learn what one of our art directors wanted. What she wanted more than anything, she said — more than a raise, more than a title, more than a business of her own, more than more responsibility or authority or recognition or meaningful assignments or leisure time — was the assurance that when her car broke down, someone would come and fix it free of charge right away without any hassle.

We made an arrangement with a local mechanic to be on call 24 hours a day, and to always have a loaner car available.

It cost the company a lot less than giving her a raise. And it made her a lot happier than getting one.

11.
NEVER LIE
ABOUT ANYTHING
IMPORTANT

*E*verybody lies. And some lies — "I don't mind, really." "Yes, I've read *Moby Dick*." "No, we're busy tonight, sorry." — are harmless.

But a lie about serious matters — about people and work and events and family — is like a cockroach: When people see one, they suspect hundreds.

If the people you work with suspect that you lie about anything that they consider important, they will not trust you.

And unless they trust you, they will not give you their hearts.

And unless you have their hearts, you cannot ideaize them.

I remember one creative director I worked for who continually lied about when we had to have work ready to present to the client. Once, an art director and I spent all weekend at the office working on a campaign that he said was needed on Tuesday, only to discover on Monday that it was not needed this Tuesday, but Tuesday next.

Suffice it to say, we did not give him our hearts.

12.
SHOW
SOME
ENTHUSIASM

Just as you enjoy working with someone who reacts with spontaneity, who bubbles, who shows pleasure in their work, so do the people you work with.

And enthusiasm, perhaps more than any other emotion, is contagious; the light you give off brightens others, the fire you set ignites others. Without it, dullness reigns.

Enthusiastic ideaists also create a mood that makes all things seem possible. Difficulties, objections, barriers, past failures, financing, regulations, defeatism, negativism — enthusiasm sweeps them all aside.

And when all things seem possible, they are possible.

That is why Emerson said, "Nothing great was ever achieved without enthusiasm."

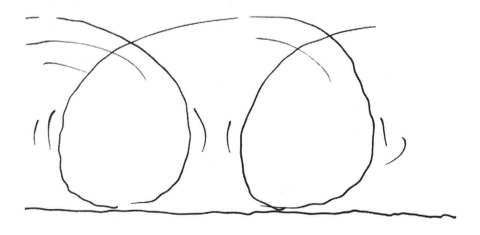

13.
ASK THEM
TO HELP YOU

Asking for help is as sure a way of making friends as lending money is of losing them.

And it's a lot more fun to work with friends than with non-friends.

Just as important, you compliment people, as John O'Toole complimented Glenn (see page 11), when you ask them to help you. You say to them that you value their judgments and their opinions.

More, you help them raise their self-images, for you are saying that you think that they are capable of making the kinds of decisions, doing the kinds of work, and handling the kinds of problems that your job requires.

Of course when you ask for help, you must either accept their suggestions or make sure they know why you reject them. To do neither defeats the whole purpose of asking for help in the first place.

14.
GET RID
OF THE WORD
"I"

"**I**" is a dividing word. It divides people into two groups — you and everybody else. And an ideaist must bring people together, not split them apart. If no nation can long endure divided, certainly no organization can.

Nor is "I" accurate when you use it to claim credit for an idea. Ray Bradbury once told me that he never knows when something he read twenty years ago will "collide" with something he read yesterday to produce a new idea for a book or a story.

In the same way, you never know who planted the seeds of the idea that grew in your mind. Was it a chance remark of your husband or wife? A sign you saw on the way to work? A comment made in a meeting? A look on someone's face? A remembrance from your childhood? A movie? A song? A poem? You owe a debt to millions for every idea, every solution, every suggestion.

Learn instead the word "we." It is more binding and accurate. And it makes working with you more fun, for it is fun for people who give credit, and fun to feel responsible for a company's success.

15.
PLAY
THE
FOOL

Ask dumb questions. Say stupid things. Be silly. Be absurd. Be illogical. Be impractical. Defend untenable positions. Challenge assumptions. Break the rules. Act like a child. Play. Take chances. Make mistakes.

When the people you work with see you doing these things, they won't be afraid to do them either.

And unless they do them, they'll never get the ideas they're capable of.

16.
HAVE
FUN
YOURSELF

Loosen up. Relax. Smile. Laugh. Enjoy yourself.

If you aren't having any fun, it's difficult for the people you work with to have any fun.

And unless they have fun, they'll never get the ideas they're capable of.

PART IV

SEVEN ORGANIZATIONAL THINGS YOU CAN DO

1.
CUT DOWN
ON
APPROVALS

As soon as one person has to ask another person for an approval, a hierarchy is created. No company can survive without such hierarchies, without checks and balances, without managers and managees.

But the more of these you create, the more your company splits into two camps — them and us, ins and outs, favored and unfavored.

Eliminate as many of these approval steps as possible.

Start with the demeaning ones, the ones that require people to get approval to spend the company's money — travel vouchers, expense reports, overtime authorizations, and so on.

Every time a person has to ask for such an approval, his or her self-image is damaged, since it says very clearly to everyone that the approver is more responsible and more trustworthy than the approvee.

And this of course is elitist rot.

Just because a person has more authority does not mean he or she is more responsible. Indeed, an argument could be made to the contrary — that the more authority people have, the less responsibly they often behave. ("Power tends to corrupt; absolute power . . .")

Because such a policy treats some people like employees and others like employers, it perpetuates the myth that some people are employees and others are employers.

In truth, none of them (unless he or she owns the company) is either. Together they *are* the company.

And you should do everything in your power to make sure that everybody — the managers, the receptionists, everybody — feel that they *are* the company. Not employees of the company. The company itself.

Requiring them to get an approval to spend what is, in effect, their own money hardly nurtures such a feeling. Instead it destroys it.

Incidentally, this is not some naive scheme that will wreck your company. It's a practical way to run a business. I've seen it work. I ran (oops — *ideaized*) a creative department quite successfully for over fifteen years based at least partly on the belief that the way to make people trustworthy is to trust them.

During that time *I never checked an expense account.*

I told the people I worked with that making them come to me for an approval irked me because it insulted their honesty. I told them that I trusted them not to rip me off, and I simply signed their expense reports without looking at them.

Certainly a few people took advantage of me. But our loss in money paled in comparison to their gain in self-image and resultant better work.

2.
MAKE
EVERYBODY
AN OWNER

The surest way to make the people you work with feel that it is their company is to *make* it their company.

After all, it is mostly the owners who drive companies. So figure out a way in which everybody who has been there at least eight months becomes an owner. That way, you'll have a company that's driven.

Of course you can do it. Hundreds of companies have. So can you.

3.

GIVE THEM WHAT THEY NEED

People don't create new ideas out of whole cloth. They create them the same way chefs create recipes for new dishes — by taking some ingredients they already know about and combining them in a new way.

The more ingredients they have to work with, the better their chances of creating something special.

The people you work with have spent a lifetime accumulating many of the ingredients they need — the broad, general knowledge about life and people and events.

You must give them the other ingredients — the specific knowledge about products and customers and competition.

Give them everything you have. And get them anything else they want.

Again, when I was ideaizing a creative department, I insisted that every writer and art director be invited to every meeting that was held on the accounts they were responsible for. An advertising agency is a meeting in progress, so I knew they could attend only those meetings dealing with creative work. Still, it sent a signal to everyone that information was the fuel for ideas.

4.
KEEP
IT
SMALL

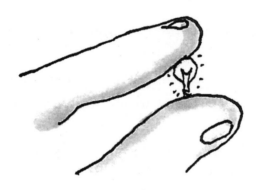

I've found that when a company has twenty-five or thirty people, most everybody seems involved with everybody else and helps everybody else. As it grows, people too often tend to pull apart and become strangers.

The founder of St. Luke's, "The Ad Agency to End All Ad Agencies" — Andy Law — agrees: "We have come to learn," he writes, "that 35 people is about as big as you can get before you cease to care about the people with whom you directly work."

Your job as an ideaist is to keep people caring for one another, to keep them together, to maintain that sense of camaraderie that helped fuel the growth in the first place.

One of the ways to do it is to organize your company so that it becomes, not a big, stranger-filled company, but a big company comprised of small companies.

This means, of course, giving more and more authority and responsibility to more and more people.

And the more you do that, the more you raise their self-images.

5.
TELL THEM EVERYTHING ABOUT THEIR COMPANY

If you expect the people you work with to come up with ideas that work, they must (a) know the problems that the ideas are designed to solve, or the opportunities that the ideas are designed to take advantage of; and (b) have the information they need to solve those problems, to take advantage of those opportunities.

So keep nothing secret, nothing for top management's eyes only.

Open up the books to them. Keep them posted on negotiations and possible mergers. Tell them of your clients' or customers' complaints.

Brief them every Tuesday morning on the state of the company. Answer their questions fully and honestly.

Tell them everything. After all, they *are* the company. They have a right to know.

6.
SHUN
RULES

Many of the great advances in the sciences and the arts — indeed, in everything — happened because people broke the rules and conventions and established new ways of thinking and doing things. Van Gogh and Picasso, Eero Saarinen and Charles Eames, Frank Lloyd Wright and Antoni Gaudí, Beethoven and Stravinsky, Pasteur and Freud, Dick Fosbury and Pete Gogolak, Gerard Manley Hopkins and e. e. cummings, Kepler and Einstein — the list could make a book.

Creative people know this, know that one of the best ways to get ideas is by breaking the rules. That's why they dislike rules and rail against them.

So make as few rules as possible.

Let them dress the way they want, and work the hours they want, and decorate their offices the way they want. If they want to work at the beach for a week, or play Frisbee in the parking lot in the afternoon, let them.

As long as what they do doesn't hurt or inhibit or offend others, what's the big deal?

Besides, who are *you* to impose rules on *them*?

It's not your company alone. It's yours *and* theirs. Together, you *are* the company.

So together you should make the rules, if any, that you need.

And — bank on it — you need fewer than you ever dreamed.

7.
PAY FOR
THEIR
EDUCATION

Time Warner, General Electric, Chick-Fil-A Foods, Johnsonville Foods, Foote, Cone & Belding, Burger King, Cumberland Farms, Mary Kay Cosmetics — these are just some of the companies, big and small, that pay for their employees' education — *whether it's job related or not.*

Join them.

Such a policy will help the people you work with accumulate more elements, more ingredients, for their idea-mills.

More, such a policy will send them a clear message that you care, not just about them doing a better job, but about them becoming richer people.

PART V

EIGHTEEN STRATEGIC THINGS YOU CAN DO

1.
DON'T ASK FOR ONE SOLUTION – ASK FOR MANY

Most people were brought up on multiple-choice and true-or-false questions, questions that have only one right answer.

So it's only natural, when you give them a problem, for them to search for the one right answer, the one right solution.

But most problems in business have no one right solution. They have many solutions. And in searching for the one right solution, people often reject good solutions, sound solutions, solutions that would work, solutions that would inspire other solutions that would work even better.

So make sure the people you work with know you want to see a lot of ideas, not just one.

Otherwise, you may never get to see the best idea they have.

2.
MAKE THEIR JOBS SEEM EASY

If you make the assignment you give people sound difficult, they will consider it difficult. And if they consider it difficult, it will be difficult.

If they consider it easy, it will be easy.

"Always think of what you have to do as easy, and it will become so," said Emile Coué.

One way to do this is to make them know, with certainty and conviction, that for every problem there are many answers, many solutions, and many ideas and that a great answer, a great solution, a great idea is already out there just waiting for somebody to grab.

Many of the experienced and good people in creative departments know this in their bones. That's why they can hardly wait for a new assignment.

But some of the younger and less-sure-of-themselves people you work with may not know it.

So instead of saying:

"I don't know if this problem's solvable, but give it a shot anyway, will you?"

Say this:

"I think there are a lot of solutions to this one. I'm sure you'll find some good ones."

3.
DON'T REJECT IDEAS –
ASK FOR MORE

Here's what my first boss, Bud Boyd, used to do:

I'd show him a proposed ad for, say, a bank, and he'd say:

"Good. Good. Let's pin it on the wall over here. Now, let's see if you can do one that's a little more impactful, one that leaps off the page."

So, I'd go away and do a simpler, bolder, more impactful ad, and he'd say:

"Good. Good. Let's pin it on the wall next to your first one. Now, do me one that will win us an award."

When I came back with what I thought was an award winner, he'd say:

"Good. Good. Now, pretend you're applying for a job in another advertising agency and the creative director there wants to see only one ad — the best ad you've ever written. Do me that ad."

The lesson Bud taught me was a simple one: There's always a better way. Always.

Perhaps Lincoln Steffens said it best. In 1931 he wrote:

"Nothing is done. Everything in the world remains to be done or done over. The greatest picture is not yet painted, the greatest play isn't written, the greatest poem is unsung."

Decades later, he's still right: There's always a better idea. Always.

So if you don't quite cotton to the ideas that the people you work with come up with, don't say:

"Those are lousy ideas. I don't like any of them."

All that does is make them doubt their abilities.

Say instead:

"OK, we've got these. Let's hold them so we don't lose them. Now, what else can we do?"

Since there's always a better idea, they very well might come up with it.

4.
GIVE THEM MORE THAN ONE PROBLEM AT A TIME

*O*ne of the best ways to get an idea is to put your unconscious to work on it.

That's what creative people in advertising agencies do all the time. If they're having trouble coming up with, say, ideas for a television commercial on a car and it isn't due until next week, they shift gears and start working on ideas for a newspaper ad on a restaurant, or a billboard on a beer.

Einstein did the same thing. So did Helmholtz and Bertrand Russell and Carl Sagan and Isaac Asimov and Thomas Wolfe and Rollo May and A. E. Housman and just about everyone else who ever wrote about getting ideas.

So if the people you work with are having trouble coming up with great ideas on a problem, tell them to forget about it and work on something else.

When they come back to the problem later, doors that were closed before will be open, barriers will be down, roads that did not exist will suddenly appear. They'll see new relationships and connections and possibilities, they'll feel new hope.

That's because, according to Michael Guillen, *CBS Morning News'* science expert, ". . . the human mind can be induced to create thoughts that come seemingly out of nowhere . . . Carl Friedrich Gauss recalled that he tried unsuccessfully for years to prove a particular theorem in arithmetic, and then, after days of not thinking about the problem, the solution came to him 'like a sudden flash of lightning.' Henri Poincaré, too, reported working futilely on a problem for months. Then one day while conversing with a friend about a totally unrelated subject, Poincaré recalled that ' . . . the idea came to me without anything in my former thoughts seeming to have paved the way for it.'"

But remember: The people you work with can't work on something else unless they have something else to work on.

Give it to them.

5.
ASK FOR
MORE IDEAS,
SOONER

If you ask the people you work with to come up with three ideas by next week, they will come up with three ideas by next week.

But if you ask them to come up with ten ideas by the end of the day, they will come up with ten ideas by the end of the day.

And many times those ten ideas will include the three ideas they would have spent all week dreaming up. Plus a couple of ideas they might have discarded, ideas that might work better than any of the others.

So raise the bar. The people you work with will find a way to jump over it.

More, they will discover the magical snowball effect of doing — doing begets doing, ideas beget ideas.

And so, almost before you know it, they'll be raising the bar themselves.

6.
IF IT ISN'T WORKING, CHANGE IT

Chemistry is a mystery.

Opposites attract. And repel. Sometimes good friends work well together. Sometimes they don't.

You never know when you put a team together if it's going to jell and become something better than its parts, or if it's going to separate and become something less than its parts.

But if something isn't working, don't compound your mistake by leaving it alone. Change it.

Just as there is always a better idea, so there is always a better team.

7.
LET
THEM
SOLO

You will never learn if people can generate ideas for themselves unless you allow them to generate ideas for themselves. So give them a chance.

Charge them with the responsibility of coming up with the solution to some problem, and see how they do. Put them in charge of something, and see how they do.

Your faith in them will make them have faith in themselves.

That is why so many people (like Harry S. Truman and Vince Lombardi) come through with flying colors when forced by circumstance to take on jobs hardly anybody thinks them capable of handling.

Don't wait for circumstances. Let them solo before they are forced to.

Let me tell you a story:

I always believed that the people who created ads or commercials should present their ads or commercials — if they wanted to — to the client.

So when Adam Kaufman, who was just "the kid in the mail room" at the time, came up with a series of wonderful radio commercials for Denny's, I asked him if he wanted to present his ideas to Barry Krantz, Denny's marketing director.

"Absolutely," he said. And off he went.

The next day, Barry called me and said: "I like the way you run a place — having faith in your young people, giving them a push, a chance. Adam's a bright young man. He did great."

Of course it could have been a failure. Even a disaster.

But if you want to help people retain their belief in their own guidance, you must take chances every now and then.

When it works, you'll not only boost *their* self-images, you might even get a boost for your own.

8.
LET THEM
DO IT
THEIR WAY

When you get in a cab, you tell the driver where you want to go, not how to get there. In the same way, ideaists should give the destination, not the route.

And when you feel sick, you tell the doctor what's wrong with you, not what medicine or treatment you need. In the same way, ideaists should state the problem, not the solution.

You must give the people you work with the freedom to take chances, to follow their own insights, to develop their own ideas, to explore roads that may not appear on the map you have in mind, to arrive at solutions you may not have thought of.

"Do it my way," are the words of an autocrat. They sap people's belief in themselves, limit their vision, and squeeze their potential.

"Find a new way," are the words of an ideaist. They restore people's belief in themselves, expand their vision, and unleash their potential.

9.
MAKE SURE
THE PROBLEM
IS THE PROBLEM

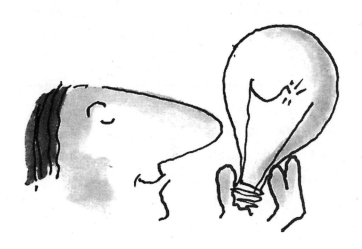

*E*instein said: "The formation of a problem is often more essential than its solution, which may be merely a matter of mathematics or experimental skills. To raise new questions, new problems, to regard old problems from a new angle, requires creative imagination and makes real advances."

For years grocers fetched groceries for their customers, and were always asking themselves: "How can I get the groceries faster for my customers?" Then somebody invented the supermarket simply by changing the question to: "How can the customer get the groceries for me?"

Henry Ford, it is said, did the same thing. He invented the assembly line simply by changing the question from "How do we get the people to the work?" to "How do we get the work to the people?"

And Edward Jenner discovered the vaccine for smallpox simply by changing the question from "Why do people get smallpox?" to "Why *don't* milkmaids get smallpox?"

If the people you work with are having trouble coming up with breakthrough answers to a problem, perhaps you asked them the wrong question and presented them with the wrong problem.

So change the question.

If you've been asking, "How do we earn more money?" try asking, "How do we spend less money?"

If you've been asking, "Why aren't people buying our products?" try asking, "Why aren't the people who do buy our products buying more of them?"

Different questions, different answers; different problems, different solutions.

10.
LET
THEM
SHINE

Make sure that the people who produce get credit for it. And make sure that they know they get credit for it.

"The deepest principle in human nature," wrote William James, "is the craving to be appreciated." Indeed, some surveys show that most workers value recognition more than money. People like to work where they know they get personal recognition for their suggestions, their efforts, their work. People like to work with someone who doesn't hold them back. And when people like to do something, they do it better.

Some leaders fear that if they allow the people they work with to shine too brightly, it will dull their own lights.

Phooey.

"Most people are advanced because they're pushed up by the people underneath them, rather than pulled up by the top," said Donald David.

After all, your hired them, didn't you? And you delegated the work to them, didn't you? And it's under your watch that they succeeded, isn't it?

11.
BE
WARY
OF FEAR

Every experienced leader knows that people often perform better when their jobs are on the line, that fear of disapproval often generates better work than the expectation of praise. Some leaders, noting this, regularly use fear as part of their leadership style.

But remember two things about the use of fear.

First, it inhibits some of the less experienced or more sensitive people, and thus prevents them from voicing their ideas. Yet because of their inexperience and sensitivity, these people often have the freshest ideas to offer.

Other people start second guessing their bosses — never a good idea when you want original thinking.

Still others become so paralyzed, they can't do anything at all.

Second, and more important, while fear is often effective in the short run, it is almost always ineffective in the long run.

Not only do good people reject working under such conditions and eventually leave, but worse — fear poisons the environment of the company, and makes working there no fun.

For these reasons, ideaists seldom use fear.

12.
MAKE IT
US VS THEM,
NOT US VS US

When you make two people or two teams responsible for the same job, too often the job will not get done.

That is why most leaders assign specific jobs to specific people or teams. It gives people a sense of responsibility and something to take pride in.

But many good people thrive on competition. Indeed, some are game-day players who only show what they can do when pressed. Knowing this, some leaders create competition within the organization in order to stimulate better work. They put two or three people, or two or three teams, on the same project, and then simply pick the best solution.

There is no denying that this system works, for it often produces more and better solutions faster, and it helps those who win believe in themselves more.

But like the use of fear, it eventually poisons the positive environment you must create. And it destroys pride, and wreaks havoc on the self-images of those who probably need help with their self-images the most.

The solution is not to eliminate competition, but to redirect it outward toward your real competitors — other companies.

When you feel that you must give an assignment to more than one person or group, make sure that those people understand that other people in other competing companies are quite possibly working on the same project, and that it is up to them to beat those other people in other companies.

This makes it a team effort — Us *vs* Them instead of Us *vs* Us — and allows you to put two or three or four people on a single project without danger of hurting either the environment or the people.

Incidentally, this kind of outwardly directed team effort happens in advertising agencies when they go after new business, and it almost invariably results in great fun, great camaraderie, and great work.

13.
SHARE WHAT EVERYBODY DOES

At The Phelps Group in Santa Monica, Joe Phelps has a "Gauntlet Wall" where the people he works with display their rough layouts and storyboards and invite everybody else to comment — to criticize, to praise, to suggest alternatives, to question.

The result? Everybody feels part of everything Joe's agency produces.

More important: Everybody knows that his or her opinion is valued and welcome. And that raises their self-images.

14.
SHARE
EXPERIENCES

When people experience something together, they share a common memory, a common insight, a common wisdom. The more of these commonalties they share, the easier it is for them to work together, for they develop a language of common experience, a language they start using when coming up with ideas:

"Remember what George said about thinking out of the box? Maybe we're in one now. Let's get out of it."

"Let's try reversing the definition."

"Let's build a benefit pyramid."

"Ah, that's just what Dr. Bronowski was talking about — how we have to look for unexpected likenesses."

As an ideaist, you must make sure the people you work with have experiences to share.

Never send any person alone to any outside conference or workshop. And when they return, make sure they report to those who didn't attend.

The first Wednesday of every month, get someone to come in at lunchtime and talk to your entire company. Shut the place down. Bring in food. Hire temps to handle the phones. Make it an event — something people will look forward to.

It will not only make working there more fun, it will make working together easier.

15.
SEARCH FOR
WAYS TO
CREATE FUN

The first Monday of every month I used to get into work even earlier than usual and spend that time thinking up ways we could have more fun at the office.

Over the years, we had scores of events — contests, outings, arts and crafts fairs, sales, displays, meals, shows, relay races in the halls, parties, concerts, cook-offs, games, family days, children days, picnics, you name it, we probably had it.

And after every one, you could sense the heightened energy, the improved morale, the increased creativity.

So get in even earlier than usual next Monday and spend the time thinking up ways you can have more fun in your workplace.

If you're having trouble coming up with ideas, just go to the bookstore. Nearly every management book you'll find there talks in some way about the importance of having fun. Many books are devoted entirely or almost entirely to the subject, books like *1001 Ways to Energize Your Employees*; *301 Ways to Have Fun at Work*; *Care Packages for the Workplace*; *Don't Go to Work—Unless It's Fun*; *Fish! A Remarkable Way to Boost Morale and Improve Results*; *Fun Works—Creating Places Where People Love to Work*; *Getting Employees to Fall in Love with Your Company*; *Making Humor Work*; *Managing to Have Fun*; and *Now, Discover Your Strengths*. Buy one. And try out some of the things they suggest.

The results will bring a smile to your face.

26.
INSIST
ON
VACATIONS

Saying that vacations invigorate people — that they help people do better work when they return — is like saying that the ocean is wet. Everybody knows it's true. And since everybody knows it, insist that everybody does it.

And remember — everybody includes you.

17.
LET THEM VACATION WHEN THEY WANT TO VACATION

There's no good time for good people to go on vacation. Whenever they take one, they'll be missed. And the better they are, the more missed they'll be.

In other words, there's no way a good person's vacation can please you. You're always going to lose in the short run, even though you know that — because of their increased productivity — the company will win in the long.

So let them take their vacations whenever it suits them best, no matter how ill it suits you.

That way, at least one of you will win in the short run, too.

18.
FORGET ABOUT EFFICIENCY, CARE ABOUT THE IDEA

Ideas are not widgets. They're not stamped out by a punch press, identical in size and shape and weight.

Each idea is a pearl — unique and fragile and luminous. And until an idea is put into action, until you see it working in the marketplace or the production line or schoolroom or the workplace, who knows what one is worth?

Their production should not be judged the way you judge a widget's either; for if you cannot immediately judge the worth of an idea, how can you judge the efficiency of the method you use to produce it?

So don't worry about efficiency.

What difference does it make if it takes ten times longer to come up with one idea than it does another? Or if one person comes up with twice as many ideas as another? Of if some people get ideas by looking out the window, others by working on a computer, and still others by reading comic books?

Don't worry about the when or the where or the how much or the how many.

Worry about the what — the idea.

WHAT SHOULD YOU DO NEXT?

With your experience, you probably have many more suggestions. Put them to use. But only if they

    (a) make working more fun, and

    (b) help people think better of themselves.

When you do these two things, you will be an ideaist, for even though you are not great enough or wise enough for people to surrender their destiny to, you will help them restore their belief in their own guidance.

To help you get started, let me tell you a story:

I used to work with an art director named Joe Forester. Every now and then Joe would step outside his office, cup his hands around his mouth, and shout down the hall at the top of his lungs — "NO SCHOOL TODAY! NO SCHOOL TODAY!

It always seemed to me that those words ought to be emblazoned on the banners of creative departments everywhere. There is something unrestrained and joyous and uplifting about them, something liberating, something that captures the essence of what kind of mind-set it takes to come up with ideas, every day.

For the creative mind-set is truly the mind-set of a child when the day is green and there is no school, and life is endless and everything is fresh and new, and nothing is impossible.

It also seems to me that NO SCHOOL TODAY gets to the heart of what this book is all about — that ideaists who shout "NO SCHOOL TODAY!" down the hallways, and companies that create a no-school-today atmosphere within the workplace, unleash the creativity of their workers.

So next time things seem a little dull and slow around your workplace, step outside your office, cup your hands around your mouth, and shout down the hall at the top of your lungs — "NO SCHOOL TODAY! NO SCHOOL TODAY!"

You'll be pleased, I think, with how it will brighten things up.

NOTES

Preface

James Webb Young, *A Technique for Producing Ideas* (Chicago: Advertising Publications, Inc., 1951).

Nathan Mhyrvold as quoted by Seth Godin in *Fast Company*, August 2000.

Part I What Is Ideaship?

Henry Miller as quoted in *Political Quotations*, edited by Daniel B. Baker (Detroit: Gale Research, 1990). Henry Miller, "The Wisdom of the Heart." 1941.

Part II.1 You help people think better of themselves

Virgil as quoted by Anthony Robbins in *Unlimited Power* (New York: Simon and Schuster, 1986).

Walter Dill Scott as quoted by Claude M. Bristol in *The Magic of Believing* (New York: Cornerstone Library, 1967).

William James as quoted by Alfred Armand Montapert in *Distilled Wisdom* (Upper Saddle River, NJ: Prentice-Hall, Inc., 1964).

Jean Paul Sartre, *Existentialism and Human Emotions* (Secaucus, NJ: Citadel Press, 1971).

Part II.2 You help create an environment that's fun

David Ogilvy, *How to Run an Advertising Agency*, advertisement, circa 1980.

Thomas J. Peters as quoted in the *Los Angeles Times*.

David Ogilvy from his address at the Chairman's Dinner, 1984, as reported in *Viewpoint* (New York: Ogilvy & Mather International, Inc., 1984).

Dave Hemsath and Leslie Yerkes, *301 Ways to Have Fun at Work* (San Francisco: Berrett-Koehler, 1997).

Alan Watts, *The Essence of Alan Watts* (Millbrae, CA: Celestial Arts, 1974).

Part III.1 Follow the golden rule

Goethe as quoted in *The Rubicon Dictionary of Positive & Motivational Quotations*, compiled by John Cook (Newington, CO: Rubicon Press, 1994).

Part III.5 Take the blame, give the praise away

The Anna Edson Taylor story as reported by Mark Sullivan in *Our Times* (New York: Charles Scribner's Sons, 1926).

Part III.6 Hire only people you like

Paul Valéry as quoted in *The New International Dictionary of Quotations* (New York: E. P. Dutton, 1986).

Part III.7 Trust them

Ralph Waldo Emerson as quoted in *The Oxford Dictionary of Quotations* (London: Oxford University Press, 1941).

Part III.8 Praise their efforts

Baltasar Gracian, *A Truthtelling Manual and the Art of Worldly Wisdom* (Springfield, IL: Charles C. Thomas, 1934).

Charles Schwab as quoted in *Quotable Business*, edited by Louis E. Boone (New York: Random House, 1999).

Reggie Jackson as quoted in *The Rubicon Dictionary of Positive & Motivational Quotations*, compiled by John Cook (Newington, CO: Rubicon Press, 1994).

John Ball as quoted by Bob Nelson in *1001 Ways to Reward Employees* (New York: Workman Publishing, 1994).

Part III.12 Show some enthusiasm

Ralph Waldo Emerson as quoted by John Bartlett in *Familiar Quotations* (Boston: Little, Brown & Co., 1955).

Part IV.4 Keep it small

Andy Law in *Creative Company: How St. Luke's Became "The Ad Agency to End All Ad Agencies"* (London: John Wiley & Sons, 1999).

Part IV.7 Pay for their education

The companies listed are from *1001 Ways to Reward Employees* by Bob Nelson (New York: Workman Publishing, 1994).

Part V.2 Make their jobs seem easy

Emile Coué as quoted by Maxwell Maltz in *Pyscho-Cybernetics* (Upper Saddle River, NJ: Prentice-Hall, Inc., 1960).

Part V.3 Don't reject ideas — ask for more

Lincoln Steffens, *The Autobiography of Lincoln Steffens* (New York: Harcourt Brace Jovanovich, Inc., 1931).

Part V.4 Give them more than one problem at a time

Michael Guillen in *Bridges to Infinity* (Los Angeles: Jeremy P. Tarcher, Inc., 1983).

Part V.9 Make sure the problem is the problem

Einstein as quoted by Anne C. Roark in the *Los Angeles Times*, 29 September 1989.

Part V.10 Let them shine

William James as quoted in *Quotable Business*, edited by Louis E. Boone (New York: Random House, 1999).

Donald David, former Dean, Harvard Business School, as quoted by James B. Simpson in *Contemporary Quotations* (New York: Thomas Y. Crowell Company, 1964).

INDEX

A

acceptance, 85-87
advertising agencies, 2, 11-12, 15–17, 6, 30, 69, 89
aloofness, 25–26
American Honda Motor Company, 43
appreciation, 103–4
approvals, 63–65
art directors, 30, 49
assignments, 83–84
attitudes, 8–13
authority, 64, 71

B

Ball, John, 43
best interests, 25–26
blame, 32–34
books, 115
Boyd, Bud, 86
Bradbury, Ray, 55

C

caring, 24–26, 71
CBS Morning News, 89
change, 9–11, 37, 93–94
commands, 28

commonalities, 112–13
company, size of, 70–71
competition, 107–9
corporate goals, 47
Coué, Emile, 84
creative departments, 2–3, 15–17, 26, 30
credit, 103–4
criticism, 22–23, 41, 42, 45

D

David, Donald, 104
Denver Republican, 34
desire, 28
destination, 98–99
doing it their way, 98–99
Dreier, Thomas, 41
dress code, 16–17, 75

E

ease of job, 83–84
education, 76–77
efficiency, 120–21
Einstein, Albert, 89, 101
Emerson, Ralph Waldo, 39, 51
enthusiasm, 50–51
environment, 13, 14–18

events, 113, 115
experiences, 112–13

F

failure, 8, 44–45
fear, 105–6, 108
five-step procedure, xi
foolishness, 56–57
Foote, Cone & Belding, 11–12
forced labor, 28
Ford, Henry, 101
Forester, Joe, 24–25
fun, 58–59, 113
    creating, 114–15
    environment, 14–18
future suggestions, 123–25

G

Gauntlet Wall, 111
Gauss, Carl Friedrich, 89–90
goals, 46–47
Goethe, Johann Wolfgang von, 23
golden rule, 21–23
Gracian, Baltasar, 41
Guillen, Michael, 89
gut feelings, 18

H

help, asking for, 52–53
Hemsath, David, 17
hierarchies, 64
hiring, 35–37

I

"I," 54–55
ideaists, 2–3. *see also* self-image
    environment and, 13, 14–18
    fun, 58–59
    self-image and, 7–13
ideas
    definition, xi
    multiple, 91–92
    multiple assignments, 89–90
    uniqueness, 120–21
    value of, xii–xiii
ideaship, 2–3
    future suggestions, 123–25
    organizational ideas, 61–77
    personal ideas, 19–59
    strategic ideas, 79–121
information, 72–73
ingredients, 69
inhibition, 106

J

Jackson, Reggie, 41
James, William, 9, 104
Jenner, Edward, 101

K

Kaufman, Adam, 96–97
Krantz, Barry, 96–97

L

Law, Andy, 71
leadership position, xii
lies, 48–49
liking people, 29–31
Los Angeles Times, 16

M

management books, 115
meetings, 69, 113
Mhyrvold, Nathan, xii
Miller, Henry, 2–3
mind-conditioning techniques,
    xi–xii
monitoring, 39
multiple assignments, 89–90
multiple ideas, 91–92

N

Napoleon, 47
needs, 68–69
no-school-today atmosphere,
124–25

O

Ogilvy, David, 15–16
organizational ideas, 61–77
O'Toole, John, 11–12, 53
ownership, 66–67, 75

P

personal ideas, 19–59
Peters, Thomas J., 15
Phelps, Joe, 111
Phelps Group, 111
Poincaré, Henri, 90
praise, 32–34, 40–43, 45
problems, 100–102
problem solving, xi, 88–90

Q

questions, 100–102

R

recognition, 103–4
rejection, 85–87
responsibility, 64, 71
results, 45
rework, 86
risk, 45
rules, 74–75

S

St. Luke's, 71
Sartre, Jean-Paul, 9
Schwab, Charles, 41
Scott, Walter Dill, 8
secrets, 73
self-image, 7–13, 37, 39, 71, 111
    approvals and, 64
    praise and, 42, 45, 53
    solo work, 95–97

sharing, 110–11
   experiences, 112–13
size of company, 70–71
snowball effect, 92
solo work, 95–97
solutions, 81–82
spontaneity, 51
Steffens, Lincoln, 86
strategic ideas, 79–121
suggestions, 53, 123–25

T

Taylor, Anna Edson, 34
teamwork, 27–28, 93–94, 107–9
treatment of others, 21–23
trust, 38–39, 49
   approvals, 64–65

U

unconscious, 89–90

V

vacations, 116–19
Valéry, Paul, 37
Virgil, 8

W

Watts, Alan, 18
301 Ways to Have Fun at Work
   (Hemsath and Yerkes), 17
"we," 55
win-win situation, 18, 33

Y

Yerkes, Leslie, 17
Young, James Webb, xi

ABOUT THE AUTHOR

Jack Foster was 18 years old and working in an insurance company with about 150 other people when he got the idea to raffle off his weekly paycheck. Fifty cents a chance to win $27.50.

The first week he made a profit of six dollars.

The next week he had collected $53 for the raffle when his boss found out what he was doing. He ordered Jack to return the money.

Then he fired him.

Ever since, Jack's been trying to come up with ideas that wouldn't get him fired.

Mostly he's succeeded.

He lucked into the advertising business 45 years ago as a writer and has been coming up with ideas ever since: Ideas for scores of companies including Carnation, Mazda, Sunkist, Mattel, ARCO, First Interstate Bank, Albertson's, Ore-Ida, Suzuki, Denny's, Universal Studios, Northrup, Rand McNally, and Smokey Bear.

During the 15 years Jack spent as the executive creative director of Foote, Cone & Belding in Los Angeles, it grew to be the largest advertising agency on the West Coast.

He also has won dozens of advertising awards including being named "Creative Person of the Year" by the Los Angeles Creative Club.

For seven years he helped teach an advanced advertising class at the University of Southern California that was sponsored by the American Association of Advertising Agencies, and for three years he helped teach an extension class at the University of California at Los Angeles on creating advertising.

Jack married Nancy ("The best idea," he says, "I ever had.") 44 years ago. They live in Santa Barbara.

ABOUT THE ILLUSTRATOR

 I was born in London, England. It was raining.

After 15 years of studying Latin I decided to go into advertising.

My first job was as an apprentice at an advertising agency called Graham and Gilles. I changed the water pots for the artists (they painted layouts with water colours in those days) and made them tea. This was before magic markers. This was even before rubber cement — I'm that old.

It was raining. It was always raining, and I was watching my favourite programme at the time — 77 Sunset Strip. I said, "Ah, sun, palm trees, women." My Dad gave me a one-way ticket.

I met Jack Foster 35 years ago at the Erwin Wasey advertising agency in Los Angeles and then again at Foote, Cone & Belding.

We worked together for about 17 years. We had a hell of a good time.

And we had a hell of a good time doing this book.